CONSIDER THE LILIES

CONSIDER THE LILIES

Meditations

Stephen M. Shick

SKINNER HOUSE BOOKS

BOSTON

This book is dedicated to the spirit of my father, Chester, who taught me to love the forest, a place where his father had toiled as a wood cutter, and to my mother, Eloise, who continues to teach me the power of reverence and devotion, gifts she received from her Christian parents. The spirit they gave me has been, time and again, awakened by Jo Ann, my loving partner, and my children—Sarah, Michael, and Dora. To them I also dedicate these words.

—*Steve Shick*

Copyright © 2004 by Stephen M. Shick. All rights reserved. Published by Skinner House Books. Skinner House Books is an imprint of the Unitarian Universalist Association, a liberal religious organization with more than 1,000 congregations in the U.S. and Canada. 25 Beacon Street, Boston, MA 02108-2800.

Printed in the United States.

Cover design by Kathryn Sky-Peck.

Text design by Suzanne Morgan.

ISBN 1-55896-463-0

Library of Congress Cataloging-in-Publication Data

Shick, Stephen M.
    Consider the lilies : meditations / Stephen M. Shick.
        p.cm.
    ISBN 1-55896-463-0 (alk. paper)
        1. Meditations. 2. Unitarian Universalist Association—Prayer-books and devotions—English. I. Title.

BX9855.S55 2003
242—dc22   2003190062

Consider the lilies of the field, how they grow;
they neither toil nor spin, yet I tell you,
even Solomon in all his glory was not clothed
like one of these.

—Matthew 6:28-29

Contents

Consider the Lilies

It is not newness we seek
    but the fresh return of the eternal.

He said, the truth is not hidden in mountains, it is not far off,
    it is in your hand, your heart, your mouth.
"So do it," he said.

He spoke in parables, mostly about money
    and the truth it can't buy.

Consider the mustard seed, he said,
    how it grows into the largest shrub.
From it, he said,
    know your true wealth and power.
Consider the birds that nest in the shrub, he said,
    how they sing in the spring.
From them, he said,
    know your true heart's song.

Consider the lilies, he said,
    and don't worry. The truth is at hand.

With the seed and the lilies
    nothing new arrives,
    and even the mockingbird
    sings songs that other birds once knew.

Nothing arrives with newness.
All is waiting to be reborn.

Please Turn

When the Lord saw that he had turned aside to see, God
called out to him from the bush.

—Exodus 3:4

Moses turned and the world changed. First he heard a voice,
then he saw the most common of things, a bush. But the bush
was burning without being consumed. The messenger, the angel
in the bush, spoke. Moses turned and then God said, "Take off
your sandals, you are on holy ground." Moses was shocked. How
could he have known that his simple turning would do so much,
would make such a difference? Again God spoke to him, saying
"I am here in the seasons of your life, in the generations of your
people. All you have to do is turn to me."

It was too much for Moses to bear, too much to look at the
presence of all that had come before him. So he hid his face.
But, having found someone who would turn, God spoke,
hoping Moses would listen. "Serve the people," God said,
"Free the oppressed and enslaved and I will be with you.
I am who I am. I am where I am. I am here."

Moses was confronted with a problem familiar to all of us
who know we stand on holy ground. If we decide to turn,
much will be expected of us, again and again. We will be
asked to free the enslaved, feed the hungry, shelter the
homeless.

Midwives and nurses know to turn the newborn's face to the mother's face so that eyes meet eyes. In this way a bond between generations is made, and the child begins to know its role and place in the changing seasons.

So much depends on turning and facing that which calls to us, knowing that we are standing on the holy ground of being.

Reflections

We have gathered,
bearing our presence,
carrying our countenance.

Like mirrors we reflect
    all we have suffered,
    all we have celebrated,
    all we have collected from life
    before arriving here.

Darkness of winter,
rebirth of spring,
abundance of autumn:
    they are with us.

We make this space sacred
by all this
and by our resolve
to project onto the pathway of tomorrow
our best reflections.

Inescapable

Where can I go from your Spirit?
Where can I flee from your presence?
　　　　　—Psalms 139:8

Haven't we always known that the Spirit lives in water,
　　　awakening, cleansing, washing away
　　　what clings to the wings of morning?

Haven't we gone alone into the empty garden, like Jesus,
　　　to talk with someone we cannot see
　　　but only feel and touch with our hearts?

Haven't we pondered the Spirit that arrives
　　　with a child,
　　　resides in a mountain,
　　　rests in a sea?

What is it we have seen riding on the back of the wind,
　　　rustling grasses, blowing leaves,
　　　touching everyone all over—again?

Why do we flee from the Spirit,
　　　hide from its longing to travel with us?

From water, from mountain, from sea,
　　　from the rush of the wind,
　　　the Spirit of Life calls:

I have known you from the beginning,
tested your resilience,
applauded your compassion.

I have searched for you
and known you.
You are wondrously made.

Bitter Cold

At the edge of the woods,
    on the coldest night of the year,
    the trees echoed the agony in my heart for
    all those who suffer and are not comforted,
    are hungry and are not fed.
A bitter cold filled the spaces between trees like
    the dark matter between stars.
Above the frozen wood even the bright-eyed moon
    shone indifferently.
Then, in a chorus of flat and sharp tones,
    the trees played a requiem on brittle wood winds.
Captured by all I could not do,
    I stopped and listened.

Blankets! Where are the blankets
    to wrap the trunks?
The coat sleeves! Where are the coat sleeves
    that I might tuck the frozen limbs into?
I don't even have enough remnants of wool
    to shelter the buds,
    the millions of buds.

Unable to help,
unable to bear the sound of this tortured wood,
    I turned away and walked toward the warm
    yellow window light of home and prayed:

Spirit of Life, God of Compassion, born in
the darkness between all that matters,
grant these loved ones mercy
from the cold, relentless winds.
    And me?
    Grant me wisdom beyond understanding.

Snow Separates

Snow separates trees, neatly dividing the hard from the soft, the vertical from the horizontal, the round from the flat. Cold divides too. Creatures burrow, nest, and cuddle, removing themselves from it. Some distinctions are clearer in February than in July. The mushy margins of the pond have turned crisp, hardening against the shore. The silent, blended green of leaves is now a webby network of barren, creaking branches. The tree, with its back to the moon, stretches clear shadows on the snow and crosses the meadow at mid-night.

We, too, often find ourselves separated. Cold things—arguments, assertions, and accusations—direct us into familiar certainties. We nestle well with our own kind. All this is good, natural, and necessary. Winter gives us permission to define where we stand, where we rest, where we burrow, or where we nest. This is being human.

But there is more to winter than separation. There is more than the contrasts that separate warm bodies. Waiting just beyond winter is the thaw point so necessary for the spring of human understanding.

In February, above the arctic circle, it is said, the sun stays out just long enough for brown algae to begin to grow. In the warmer months this algae will help bring life to the frozen winter sea. Winter is the time when miracles of growth and unity take shape.

Excavating Joy

How exactly good it is to know myself in the solitude of winter.

—Wendell Berry

Archeologists know how difficult it is to trace life in shifting sediments. The amateur finds objects and rejoices. The professional looks for the context. In winter I have excavated life like an amateur and found joy.

Each vanishing layer of snow reveals memories. The melting first layer releases the bent top of a hemlock sapling and speaks of tenderness frozen into a torturous pose. Further melting exposes a turquoise ball and tells of a child's play interrupted.

Today's retreating snow reveals the footprints of a giant. I smile, knowing something of this lighthearted beast. His trail is nearly straight and runs from my kitchen door to the compost pile seventy-five feet away, a good distance for most of the mammals that traverse the snow this close to the house. This was no small creature. The footprints, separated by four or five feet, indicate a walking stride of two to three feet.

I smile, then laugh, remembering a deep-winter moment in the kitchen. The sun was shining brightly through the windows, when I noticed that the compost had outgrown its plastic container by the sink.

I took off my socks, rolled up my pant legs, and grabbed the compost, pausing only long enough to stuff the morning's orange peels down into the primal ooze. I opened the creaking door and the race was on. I got off to a slow start, but after clearing the ice on the porch steps, I was crossing the yard with giant strides.

The crow in a nearby tree must have been laughing heartily as he watched my tender feet sink into the snow and spring up only to sink quickly down again and again. The next day I would discover the scratches on my legs where the frozen crystals had bitten, but for those few minutes I was in flight and fulfilling a ritual I have enjoyed for years—a brief, barefoot run in the snow.

At the compost pile there was no pausing to contemplate the "dust-to-dust" nature of its composition, no boot-warm musing at the crystal patterns on a potato skin or the color of orange-peel mold. With one quick gesture the plastic container was emptied of its offerings and I was leaping back to the warm sunshine of the kitchen.

I wiped my red feet dry with laughter. An exhilarating joy filled my heart as I did a silly dance for a second or two.

The melting snow reveals a joyful moment experienced in the depth of winter and it is still "exactly good."

Winter Tomatoes

I love winter, but by February I am sorely tempted to forsake it altogether. What a fickle lover I am when I go into the basement to plant tomato seeds. I am easily distracted from the task at hand by thoughts of the warm breeze that will blow on that May day when I set the young plants in the ground. While sowing the Rutger's tomato seeds a fraction of an inch under the soil, my mind rushes forward and sees healthy tomatoes ripening on the vine. Then I journey back in time to when I first learned that this strain of seed produced my father's favorite tomatoes. I may even walk into the adjacent room, where a picture of my father's father hangs on the wall. He is kneeling next to a bumper crop of tomatoes. In the midst of all this I will find it hard to focus on how good it is to plant tomatoes in my basement in wintertime.

Forsaking dreams and memories, I harness myself to the moment and the task. Holding a tiny tomato seed on my fingertip, I encounter wonder and adoration. Here, neatly contained, is the tangle of vines whose fragrance will enchant me in summer. It's a wonder that the transformation will happen at all and more so that it will be so effortless and precisely predictable.

Wonder then gives way to awe. Millions of tomatoes whose generations span life itself brought me this one tiny seed. All that needs to be done has been done by a force beyond my imagination.

What, I ask, is this experience of planting tomato seeds all about? Memory and dreams certainly are part of it. Albert Schweitzer called it "reverence for life," and from it, he said, all human ethics naturally grow. In the moments I recognize this I know I am in love.

With seeds now moistening in their containers, I carry them upstairs. Placing them near a warm and sunny window, I know how good it is to be in winter knowing all is safe in the seed.

To Flame

All that we need is here now.

From the ages of the earth
  we have gathered energies
  in wood, coal, oil,
  and other remnants of life.

And the air, it is here too,
  and it need not be pure.

All is ready,
  here,
  in the dark.

Will you strike yourself
  against life's hard surfaces
  and let the flame out,
  or let it be born from your giving,
  let it be eternally released

  to spread the light?

Changing Seasons

This being human is a guest house.
Every morning a new arrival.

> —Rumi

The "guest house" metaphor rests uncomfortably on the modern mind. We like to think we are more like private mobile homes. We can open and close doors at will, all the time moving in the direction we choose. We are not flophouses taking in whoever comes. We are in control of our destiny.

And yet we soon become disillusioned, resentful and self-pitying when we believe that we are in charge of nearly everything that happens to us. Living day in and day out with this expectation is not good training for the times when life suddenly turns sour. Death, illness, and physical and psychological suffering come as thieves in the night, robbing us of the illusion that we can keep emotions out once they have invited themselves in. At the end of a day filled with the good things of life, we go to bed satisfied and content, and yet we wake up anxious and fearful the next morning. A pestering health concern arrives unannounced and even those of us who generally dismiss such things find ourselves motionless and imagining the worst, wondering what will happen to the family if we die—not someday but today. How quickly we can become locked inside our temporarily immobile homes with the visiting fear of our own mortality.

We can analyze our uninvited guests psychologically, study their sociological characteristics, and examine them chemically or biologically. Through all that we can gain insight, but we are still left with the simple fact that these guests are always arriving, always traveling with us. Rumi implores us to "welcome and entertain them all."

Among the Trees

You were among the trees today;
>how your countenance had changed.

You whispered sweetly of peace
>in the warmth of summer.

You wooed us with kindness,
>caressed us with your longings.

How we trusted you.

But today there is no gentleness in your ways, no pleasures in
>your presence.

You blow cold indifference across our bodies.

From yesterday's snowflakes,
>you've fashioned shards of crystal to pierce skin,
>shatter bones.

The woods now speak of what you did here
>before we came to this place hungry for solace.

Here you trapped the deer in your pure snow and
>called the wolves and bears that they might satisfy
>their hunger.

There was no peace in your presence then. There is none now.

You have tortured the trees, torn them limb from limb.

In the deep freeze, while you bask on southern shores, we've
>heard them
>cry as you lift their sinew from their bone.

We can trust your peace no longer.
We will no longer be deceived.

We see you more clearly now
        than when we first arrived in this wood.
We will go now from your presence,
        mindful of this,
        and in the stillness of our homes,
        light fires from the embers
        of our smoldering hearts.

Beyond Passing Seasons
In memory of Joe and Eleanor Miller

⎯☙

There is no less magic now,
no less mystery now,
than when your comet first caught our eye.

Crossing seasonal space you captured
      from cold indifference, sparks of hope,
      from weary stillness, light waves of resilience,
      from the dark, the light of distant stars
            that once burned bright and also died.

Looking where you passed
      will not reveal your eternal radiance.

But look further—
      out there beyond seasonal change,
      deep in the galaxies of the human spirit,
      flares of passion have been released
            to shape justice
            and move the world toward peace.

An Unfolding

A purple bud appeared. Shaped like a pea, it became visible weeks ago on the slender stem of the *Phalaenopsis,* my first orchid. I had carefully placed the plant in a shaded area of a very sunny room and watered and misted it, praying that what I was doing was not the "too much" that the greenhouse employee cautioned me about.

For weeks I watched two stems extend themselves under the large oblong leaves. Then, along their lengths, deep purple joints formed where the buds would emerge. Weeks passed before I noticed the small head of a third stem, greener than the two now turning dark purple. By the time it reached half of the length of the older stems, the petals of the oldest bud opened into five soup-spoon shapes, a royal flush. The two petals in front were convex and the three in back concave, and all were light purple fading toward white. In the center piece, purple lines accentuated the plant's private parts.

I tried watching the unfolding, but found this as impossible as watching my children leave childhood behind or watching the wrinkles on my own face deepen. Something was happening that I could not control. Still, I tried to watch, not in the hope that I could slow down the transformation but because it slowed me.

Nature provides a certain gift for all impatient watchers. I knew this bud would open soon, maybe in the morning.

Still, when it happened, the grandeur of its beauty came as a glorious surprise.

The gift of surprise can also come when you are not watching. That morning, while looking at the orchid, I heard a sound echoing through the woods. "They're back!" I exclaimed. My whole heart lifted, as if some keeper of an inward dam had flung the spillway gate wide open. The sound was that of the giant pileated woodpecker crafting a nest somewhere high and out of sight.

The surprise of one miracle while watching the slow unfolding of another makes for a good day.

The Blessing

In memory of Virginia Bernard

꧁

Listen, the night rain has filled the cupped tulip,
  every drop a gift—people, purposes, pains, and promises,
  knowledge, wisdom, and compassion.
In the night the brimming cup has spilled
every drop, an offering—
  friends, fellowship, futures, and fulfillment,
  insights, visions, and commitment,
  loves felt and lives lived.

The rich, dark earth soaks up
every drop, a tearful blessing,
  nameless now,
  that surrenders, saturates, and satisfies.

Listen, in the wet dawn, to the enduring rain.
every drop falls in the eternal breeze that
  brought the rain,
  filled the cup,
  made the offering, gave the blessing.

Resurrection Naturally

Perhaps you have heard of the *Triops,* a small crustacean native to the American Southwest. The eggs of these amazing creatures can do what none of us can but what all of us are called to do again and again. With the ability to dry up, die, then come back to life, they are life's resurrection miracle. The period between their death and rebirth can be decades, or hundreds or thousands of years. By releasing all their water they enter a state between death and life. What should we call it? Living? The twilight zone? Or just waiting and hoping?

There is a great diversity of body shapes among the unhatched creatures who perform this long waiting for rebirth. Scientists have done unspeakable things to test the faith of these resurrectionists. Even after they are dangled outside of a space shuttle and exposed to the cold and radiation of outer space, they come quickly back to life when baptized in water.

These creatures confirm what we have long suspected: Resurrection is natural. All it requires is patience followed by the nurturing touch of water or, in the case of humans, the loving touch of another person.

Waiting

Too long have we sat in darkness.
Too long have we waited for your touch,
    your fingers to caress
    wrinkled brows smooth.
When will you lead us to the balm in Gilead,
    to the elixir that renews,
    to the shaman who can draw out the sickness that grows
        in your absence?
And if not you, then who?
    Will she rise from the earth and
    break the frozen ground of spring
    that holds us down, motionless?

    Will he rise from the simplicity of death
    and fulfill the promise you gave him?

How long must we wait?
Yet while we wait you have already arrived.

You have brought with you
    the balm,
    the elixir,
    the shaman,
    mother earth,
    your only son,
    and released them
    into our deepest longing.

Rich Earth

In earth rich with memory, love, and hope,
spring is gathering seeds of justice.

One in a million
sinks roots deeply
into the damp soil of ancient struggles
and grows a giving tree.

One in a million
drives shoots upward
through mulch of decaying leaves and wood
to sway in stormy winds.

One in a million
grows strong enough to stand
    in the baking heat of cruel oppression,
    in the raging floods of wasted abundance.
Outstretched and uplifted
branches hold firm
the wounded songbird
long enough for wings to heal
and risk flight again.

In forests of glory,
dead limbs and trunks fall
into the rich earth,
where spring
gathers seeds of justice.

For Now

We gathered in the yard facing the tidal water. The open tent framed the blue New England sky. The couple's eyes, like the noonday sun, sparkled with deep assurance and hope. We knew that this couple walking down the aisle between white folding chairs had traveled distances none of us knew. His body, young and crippled by disease, was steadied by a polished cane, a well-worn part of his wardrobe. Her body, young and strong, moved gracefully with the rhythm of his courage. They carried with them that day the sobering news of yesterday: He had been diagnosed with yet another disease.

There was no pretense here, no feigned happiness for the sake of gathered loved ones. From victorious hearts they had crafted their vows. He recited a lighthearted verse he had penned with love, and she wove a profound literary tapestry of hope. They created a communion of all spirits as they gathered flowers from their families and remembrances and blessings from all who had gathered.

Weddings are always celebrations of hope, and there are always secrets that test a couple's courage. Yet at some weddings you can glimpse wisdom and bravery and know that true beauty is created on the crucible of pain; that hope grows best in dark, rich soil; that happiness is not "forever after" but here and now; and that you may not control the circumstances of your life but you can choose how you will live.

Sacred Places

Where the prairie rolls onto the shore of Pasha Spa in the Black Hills of South Dakota, there is a hole in the ground. The hole is called Wind Cave because of the whistling noise that comes from it. When the air pressure is low outside the wind rushes out in a stream strong enough to blow your hat off; when the pressure is high, it rushes in. The cave has been doing this type of blowing and sucking for millions of years. In 1903 it became the seventh national park and the first cave to be so designated, a distinction that pales in significance to an earlier honor bestowed upon it by a Lakota creation myth. From this hole or one like it, it is said, the buffalo, humans, and other creatures emerged and began roving the prairies.

On a recent tour of the cave, one visitor wondered aloud, "Did the Lakota people ever use the cave?" "No," the guide said. "They considered it sacred and would not enter." The discussion ended with no exploration of the intriguing subject of why some humans place limits on where they can go and others do not.

Not far from the Wind Cave there is another beautiful place, a series of granite spires known as The Needles. Once gold was discovered among the pinnacles, our government decided to abandon an agreement that allowed the original occupants to keep these majestic peaks sacred. Tunnels were carved through the towering gray giants and now pour cars and buses into this once sacred space.

Mother Earth has no private areas where she can simply be. Rather, we believe, she must always be of use to her children.

Our insatiable hunger to possess a certain kind of wealth leads us to dig holes in a once sacred mountain and probe a once sacred cave simply because they are there.

But when nothing is sacred then perhaps everything becomes profane. We are still like children desperately crying out for limits.

Monuments

On this green bank, by this soft stream,
    We place with joy a votive stone,
That memory may their deeds redeem,
    When, like our sires, our sons are gone.
               —Ralph Waldo Emerson

A green heron stands motionless on the bank of Emerson's soft stream. In its beak it holds a fish, just the right size for this small cousin of the great blue heron. A feather-warming breeze rustles the nettles and the shoreline jewel weeds nod.

The votive stone still stands not far away, asking us to remember those who died here on the first day of the American Revolution.

My mind is disturbed by the gentle mingling of bird, water, fish, and history. Behind the heron is another sign. Perhaps you've seen one like it. No artist carved its design or chiseled its inscription. No poet was commissioned to write a hymn for the installation. Instead, unceremoniously placed, a bare steel shaft is imbedded in mud. It holds a rectangular sign with the international warning symbol emblazoned over the picture of someone fishing. The stenciled words call to us for a new revolution. They read: "Warning: Mercury. Don't eat the fish."

Balance at the Water's Edge

Wading at the water's edge, a spirited young mother was squeezing the last drop out of summer. A bare-bottom toddler was riding on one hip, and a four-year-old had an arm locked around her neck. Amazed and wanting to applaud, I watched her enjoyment flow. The balance seemed perfect. Then the hip rider slipped. In a single motion almost too quick to see, the mother tightened her grip on the slider, swung her opposing arm and hip, loosened her four-year-old's neck lock, and guided him gently into the water. Everything seemed under control again. Then, unexpectedly, she lost her footing and began to stagger backward. It was at this instant that a young man standing nearby reached out to steady her.

Multitasking is risky business even when your passion is fully engaged and your instincts good. The young mother knew instinctively when to loosen the grip on one child, secure the grip on the other, and accept help. How fortunate, and how wise.

Late Summer Rain

Listen, O drop, give yourself up without regret, and in exchange gain the Ocean.

—Rumi

I couldn't help myself. The rain had been falling all night, sometimes gently and sometimes throwing itself against the roof and windows. The soaking was making me more pliable, softening my resolve and inhibitions. From the window, mesmerized, I watched individual drops splash on the ground, creating miniature fountains. Once together they gathered in ever expanding pools with possessive shorelines. I felt a quiet fall into me. I floated free from my "to do" list, free from the old parental moorings to not "go out in it" or to "come in before you catch cold."

I prepared quickly by donning a raincoat and grabbing an old shower curtain from the garage. As I approached the woods, the sound of falling rain was as enchanting as a siren's shoreline song. Not far into the trees I found a good place to sit. I carefully unfolded the shower curtain in a way that I hoped would keep the rain off my bottom. Seated, I pulled the corners up over my folded legs. I was no longer an outsider looking at the rain from a dry, comfortable room. Now I was in the middle of it, watching from the inside. Several young white pine trees formed an irregular line ahead of me. A diamond-clear raindrop seemed to be suspended from each needle cluster. Together the trees' needles and the water formed a different kind of curtain. Its green transparency was comforting.

I had always thought of the word *rain* as a singular thing, like an ocean, a pond, a sea. "Look at the rain," I would say, as though rain were one. Directly to my right and about eyebrow high, was a long branch of a maple sapling. It reminded me of what I knew all along but had lost in language. Rain is billions of individual drops of water, each with its own destination and timing. Some of these drops hit the large leaves of the sapling as a mallet pounds a marimba, but sometimes the drops fell with a light touch, sometimes quickly, sometimes drawn out, but always individually. I mused that rain is to raindrops as music is to individual tones: a fluid outpouring of linked individuality.

But something else became clear. The distance each drop traveled before arriving on earth is enormous. I found it strangely comforting and refreshing to imagine myself a drop in an ocean of sky.

Arrival of Hope

For Mekinsey Shick, born November 26, 1993

⁓

On winter's dawn she has come,
    rising in our hearts,
    spreading warmth
        on our coldest fears.

Who is she?
    An epiphany?
    A gift of time claimed from chaos?
    A mystery dissolved into tiny features,
    A face, feet, fingers?

We gaze into her eyes,
    and we see
    years of joy and sorrow.
We listen to her heart,
    and we hear the rhythm
    that connects us.
We touch her softness with our souls.
Steadily, this daughter of grace reveals us.
Firmly, the bud is set for spring.

Communion with Earth and Sky

Early spring awakens
memories of a deeper cold
and hopes of a warmer wetness,
sprouting seeds and budding branches.

Gray trees on gray sky screen eyes
from all that lies waiting:
      the color of a million flowers,
      the feathers of migrating songbirds,
      the blossoming smiles of friends.

Soon we will no longer look to the night stars to guide us.
Soon the path will be lit and our task certain.

In the warming days we will plant our future,
      uprooting useless skeletons of last year's harvest,
      breaking the clods of indifference,
      carefully pulling the weeds of neglect
         so that roots can stretch.

Before the harvest moon rises and we wait again,
      images of still distant summer days
      awaken thoughts of a time when
      all is done that can be done.

Then the harvest.
Then the transformation.
Then the baking.

Then the bread.

All we know and love is in this cycle.
All that has been or will be is in this loaf.
Take it.
Break it.
Give thanks
     and pass it on.

Vespers

Spirit of Life, God of Love,
in twilight
between day and night,
we sense your presence among us.

We remember
     the promise of the morning,
     the dancing brightness of noonday,
     the lengthening shadows of the hours just past.

Like the dusk, we too live between action and reaction,
     our lives growing in the spaces that separate.
Here we make our life choices,
     shaping the way we enter and emerge from the darkness.

Spirit of Light,
grant us wisdom to value your half-light,
     where all is not clear
     but all is done for now,
     and we can rest.

Reinforcements

I had a colleague once who was a historian with the uncanny ability to describe our shared circumstance in a way that often released the tension of the moment. When I would become frustrated by the growing pains of our common enterprise he would provide a reassuring and flattering perspective. "We are in the same moment," he would say, "as the Union Army was at Gettysburg right before the reinforcements arrived."

I began practicing viewing my own life as a historian might. When I felt particularly stressed I would get up from my desk, walk to the corner of the room, and watch myself at work. Often I would find myself laughing fondly at the man hunched tensely over his desk. Then I would briefly narrate the situation. This little exercise helped me to step outside of my self-centered view of the world.

In our troubled world I am finding more need to be a disciplined observer of my own life. This is not an escape but a prerequisite for being more fully engaged in all the public and private dimensions of life.

One restless day I sought comfort in a grove of beech trees. In the yellow light of this sanctuary I said to myself, "There sits Steve Shick." The rustling leaves applauded (so much for modesty). "Steve," I said, "has a loving partner and three children who love him. His mother is still alive, well, and happy."

Before I could say another word a quietness began moving through me. It was as though the wind were lifting my tensions away; I could practically hear their fleeting footsteps in the dry leaves.

The restlessness that had taken me to that yellow spot among the trees had been stilled. Within a few minutes the wildlife I had frightened away returned. The blue jays swooped around me, and the chipmunks and squirrels scurried and rummaged. I took off my shoes and stayed a while longer. When I got up I felt renewed. The reinforcements had arrived.

Journey Inward

⟋୰

The sky was brightening over the snow. Comfortably indoors, I looked up from my study of Buddhism and Christianity to watch a flock of slate-colored juncos flit in and out of a juniper.

Focused again, I came across words that moved my spirit. These words had been lost for nearly two thousand years. Mohammed Ali, the Bedouin digger of birdlime fertilizer, not the great boxer, found them with many others that had been buried in the Egyptian desert by Gnostics.

Gnostics have been described as Zen Christians who were more interested in observing and experiencing the kingdom than writing about it or believing in it. For three hundred years before Jesus arrived, Buddhists, among others, had been seeding the region with such thoughts. The particular words I read were from the Gospel of Thomas. They challenged me to pause and go deeper: Jesus said, "If you bring forth what is within you, what you bring forth will save you. If you do not bring forth what is within you, what you do not bring forth will destroy you."

Both Jesus and Buddha taught the importance of regularly taking an inward journey to find what will save you. The gifts buried inside each of us, they said, are more valuable than wisdom sealed in any book, captured in any creed, or observed in snow, leaves, birds, or sky. Four lessons emerged from my morning's encounter with this ancient text.

Whatever you find on your inward journey should not be generalized. Your journey is your own. To know this is to know that others too can discover wisdom that shows them how to live compassionate and loving lives.

The gift you have inside is universal. Jesus said, according to the Gospel of John (perhaps another Gnostic text), "I am the way, the truth and the light." Some Christians have used this to drive a wedge of absolutism between believers and those who follow other religious paths. If John is interpreted in light of the unearthed Gnostic texts, however, then Jesus begins to sound a whole lot like a Zen master, in whom the "living Buddha" is reborn as a guide for others who are willing to take an inward journey.

"What is not brought forth can destroy you" is a cautionary note. On your inward journey you may discover, for example, the "child within." If you do not let that child out to innocently and enthusiastically embrace life, your spirit will wither.

The Gospel of Thomas states, "If you bring forth what is in you, what you bring forth will save you." The inward journey is not beyond time but in the here and now. When you bring forth what is inside you, your true self, you will be saved from whatever distracts you.

My morning's encounter with ancient texts, the brightening sky in late autumn, and the flitting juncos encouraged me to faithfully continue my inward journey.

Life Hangs a Wire

It seems as if the wire had touched the chaotic liquid and crystallization had begun. It seems to me that nature wears a new aspect and life has got a new meaning since I came hither.

—Theodore Parker

Sometimes the shore water speaks, wave upon wave gently opening us. The ocean winds whisper too of things unseen, then rush away. They kiss the dune grass in summer and slide across the thin lips of ice on a tidal pool in winter.

Our bifurcated worldview sees such images detached from struggles for peace and social justice. The real world, we say, is not a walk on a beach but a flood of pain and suffering, not a romantic breeze but a whirlwind of destruction.

Theodore Parker, the fiery nineteenth-century Unitarian abolitionist was both mystic and activist. He saw unity where we often discern separation. One observer at the time noted it was impossible to disassociate him from the earth, which revealed to him the divine nature of everything. Early in his life Parker pledged that he would preach only about things he had experienced inwardly.

His encounter with the natural world shaped his vision of justice. While serving his first congregation in the ocean community of Barnstable, Massachusetts, he had a transformative seashore experience. "He tramped the sand dunes and the shore," the historian Henry Steele Commager writes, "and the grandeur of nature seemed to liberate his mind."

Parker's liberation from the religious and social orthodoxy of his day was connected with the confidence and identity he experienced in nature.

Each day, he thought, life hangs a wire before us, waiting for us to touch it to the liquid center of our being, where crystallization can begin.

Silent Looking

Now, He thought, there should be a sky over their heads so
they can look up at it.

—Seneca creation story

The windows in the ceiling of my living room frame the sky.
One day's picture drew me upward along the branches of
two mature oak trees, past leaves of green and mustard
yellow and onto the outer reaches of a swaying mobile of
branches. Looking up aimlessly, in silence, I saw art.

I saw more while spending a morning in an art museum.
Here, looking without thought is encouraged. I arrived
with a talkative and light-spirited bunch of ministers. As we
entered the museum we became quiet. Strangely, all the
eloquence we so value professionally became irrelevant.
While walking the exhibits in pairs, groups, or individually,
we didn't speak much at all. We quietly looked at the paint-
ings, letting ourselves be drawn to reverence by artistic
expressions of the human spirit. After the visit we regaled
each other with our words of description and impressions
of meaning.

A deep feeling of being alone is often the price we pay for
silent looking. Perhaps that is why we so rarely quiet our
mind, why we fill our houses, cars, shopping malls, restau-
rants, offices, and elevators with wall-to-wall sound. It's hard

to tap that primal feeling when the senses are overloaded with stimuli. In a sense all the noise of our modern world protects us from that feeling.

If you are willing to pay the price of silence you can begin to actually feel life, or the presence of God. Silent looking is at the center of religious awareness and practice. Enter an empty church, synagogue, temple, mosque, or other sacred landscape and you will quickly be drawn into silent looking (a high window will also do the trick). You may at first feel the absence of words or sounds, but soon the presence of something more important will arrive.

It's not easy or comfortable to risk silent looking. Luckily, there is a sky over our heads to remind us and reassure us that it is good to be still and to look.

Bitter Grapes

My grandmother said, "Life is bitter grapes." Yet she was a positive woman, strong, determined, and pleasant. She gained much of her strength from her deep Christian faith and probably didn't realize that her statement about the nature of life was also an affirmation of the first truth of Buddhism: Life is suffering. To be aware and alive is to know that life is bitter and sweet. My grandmother and the Buddha found contentment and smiled, knowing well the bitter side of life.

With hands gnarled with arthritis, my grandmother loved to play the piano for me while I sang. Her skin, transparent and thin, would flex with what must have been her determination to play through the pain. We are all called upon to play through the pain. The music of life demands a response. The writer of Deuteronomy knew this well. "I set before you this day blessing and cursing, therefore choose life." He did not say choose life only when you are free of pain and trouble. Nor did he say choose life and you will be spared from pain and trouble. Rather, he said, choose life so you and those who follow you may live.

The Rangeway

A decade ago we moved into a small house with the address 27 Rangeway. The house overlooked a path, an old colonial stone fence, and a stream. At the margin of the path the previous owners had created a small organic garden, a strip of tilled soil at the sunny edge of the woods. They had spoken regretfully of having to leave the garden behind.

One year they returned and brought us a surprising gift. "It doesn't belong in our new place," they said. The gift was an arrowhead they had found years ago while digging in their garden. Handing it to us, they said, "It belongs here."

This treasure is only two inches long, flat on one side and convex on the other, brown-gray except in four places where the black flint is exposed. It calls me to imagine the comfort others must have found here before the land was cleared, before the stone fence and the house were built, and before the path was trodden. I received this offering humbly. Then, fighting the desire to have and to hold, I pledged to pass it on to whoever lives on this land next. In the meantime, the arrowhead is on display in our living room.

When I touch the arrowhead an image comes to me—a family, perhaps a dozen people, living on this land. In deep concentration a young man sat at the edge of the campsite, carefully striking stone on stone, giving just the right shape to the object now in my hand.

I have seen deer, foxes, turkeys, young and old bikers, and eager and tired hikers travel this rangeway—each, for a moment, belonging to this particular place where time and memories pass as guests and deep longings beckon them to return or stay.

At the Margin

At the margin of a newly cut field,
where every blade still stands secure,
where every bud is fearless now,
a lily
> turns to the dawn
> > and opens.

Here, in the kingdom of the living,
> danger has passed,
> and clustered buds,
> moist and swollen,
> choose their day.

We too grow at the margins,
where our fear of cutting is faced,
where we accept our lowly place,
where we explode in the dawn,
> with the brilliance
> > of a flower.

Making Sacred

Here we have gathered the elements of our lives.
Aware and unaware,
we have carried them to this place—
  the joy of waking and living,
  the pleasure found in meaningful work,
  the blush of health,
  the pain of illness,
  the grief of loss,
  and the gift of love.
Some of these we have carried a long way.
Some have bent our backs until our eyes
  could no longer see the horizon.
Some have carried us upward with purpose,
  feathered wing in flight.

All we have carried through the seasons of our lives
has brought us here
to this place we make sacred
by our coming together
and reciting these gathering words:

Come, you are welcome here.

A Seasonal Haggadah

How many and wondrous are the favors of your seasons.

Had you brought us out of the hunger of winter
    and not fed us on the promise of spring,
it would have been enough.

Had you fed us on the promise
    and not given us the Sabbath of summer,
it would have been enough.

Had you given us the summer's Sabbath
    and not brought us to the harvest,
it would have been enough.

Had you given us the harvest
    and not renewed the cycle of the seasons,
it would have been enough.

Had you given us renewal
    and not challenged us with the prophets of righteousness,
it would have been enough.

Had you given us the prophets of righteousness
    and not come to us again,
it would have been enough.

To Look

The doer looks
with a focused gaze
upon a row of things once made,

or, if of the reformer's mind,
reshapes the things
to fit the times.

But the watcher looks
in another way
and sees the commonplace
of day
      a radiance on a wilted flower,
      a nest in a cathedral tower.

The watcher moves with a deliberate gait
and knows the power of the wait
      to lift the weariness of time
      and show the world as a holy shrine.

Enough Said

Spirit of Life, God of Love.

I have said much, perhaps too much,
about my quiet visits
to the mirror waters

> where you rest in me,
> where I have floated gracefully like a deeply anchored
> lily,
>> where I have suspended my weighty matters on
>> the surface of your depths,
> where I have called out, "Why do I speak at all?"

I have said much, perhaps too much,
about feeling the flow of your love

> as you surge through my veins, pulse through my brain,
> as you extend my hand to serve and awaken others,
> as you prophetically echo the dream whose seed was
>> planted long ago
>>> in the garden.

I have said much, perhaps too much,
and now without a word,

I rest in you.

About the Author

After a career in community ministry as a radio broadcaster and social activist, Stephen Shick entered parish ministry in 1997 and currently serves the Universalist Unitarian Church of Haverhill, Massachusetts. He is author of *Just Congregations* and his social and religious writings have appeared in a variety of publications, including *How We Are Called*, *The Communion Book*, and *UU World*. Shick has three children—Sarah, Dora, and Michael—and lives with his partner, Jo Ann, in Lexington, Massachusetts.

Unitarian Universalist Meditation Manuals

Unitarians and Universalists have been publishing annual editions of prayer collections and meditation manuals for 150 years. In 1841 the Unitarians broke with their tradition of addressing only theological topics and published *Short Prayers for the Morning and Evening of Every Day in the Week, with Occasional Prayers and Thanksgivings*. Over the years, the Unitarians published many volumes of prayers, including Theodore Parker's selections. In 1938 *Gaining a Radiant Faith* by Henry H. Saunderson launched the current tradition of an annual Lenten manual.

Several Universalist collections appeared in the early nineteenth century. A comprehensive *Book of Prayers* was published in 1839, featuring both public and private devotions. During the late 1860s, the Universalist Publishing House was founded to publish denominational materials. Like the Unitarians, the Universalists published Lenten manuals, and in the 1950s they complemented this series with Advent manuals.

Since 1961, the year the Unitarians and the Universalists consolidated, the Lenten manual has evolved into a meditation manual, reflecting the theological diversity of the two denominations. Today the Unitarian Universalist Association meditation manuals include two styles of collections: poems or short prose pieces written by one author—usually a Unitarian Universalist minister—and anthologies of works by many authors.